THE OFFICIAL
NEWCASTLE
UNITED
ANNUAL 2020

Written by Mark Hannen
Designed by Jon Dalrymple

Thanks to Michael Bolam,
Stan Gate and Paul Joannou.

A Grange Publication

© 2019. Published by Grange Communications Ltd., Edinburgh, under licence from Newcastle United Football Club. Printed in the EU.

Photographs © Serena Taylor and Getty Images

ISBN 978-1-913034-26-9

CONTENTS & WELCOME

WELCOME TO THE OFFICIAL NEWCASTLE UNITED ANNUAL 2020.

The 2018/19 season was a bit of a rollercoaster season for United, which eventually ended with a mid-table finishing position, helped by being the last team to beat champions Manchester City back in January 2019!

Hopefully the 2019/20 season will be one to be enjoyed by everyone who supports this great club. From everyone at Newcastle United, thank you for you loyal and incredibly passionate support. Enjoy the read.

We're ready to go! Kit and boots await the arrival of the players to the changing room.

Martin Dúbravka receives his player of the season award (2017/18) from United's Swedish fan club.

A typical Geordie welcome from the Gallowgate End for new signing Miguel Almirón prior to his home debut against Huddersfield Town.

Dusk at St. James' Park with the lights on in this picture from behind the boards in the Gallowgate south-west corner.

Wonderful to have the early 70s strike duo of Malcolm Macdonald and John Tudor together again on the St. James' Park pitch.

The United shirt proudly bears the 'United as One' logo, a new brand identity to link all of the club's work in the fields of diversity, inclusion and welfare.

In November 2018 the club unveiled a new memorial to those United personnel who lost their lives in the Great and Second World Wars.

The huge flag, by 'Wor Flags', 78m x 54m, the biggest to be unveiled at any European football stadium, makes its bow against Liverpool.

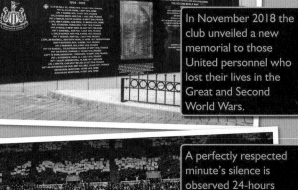

A perfectly respected minute's silence is observed 24-hours before Armistice Day as United prepare to take on Bournemouth.

On the fiftieth anniversary of United winning the Fairs Cup, John Craggs, Keith Dyson, Alan Foggon and Bob Moncur returned to Budapest, the scene of their triumph.

A ROLLERCOASTER CAMPAIGN FOR UNITED

After securing a top ten finish in May 2018, Newcastle United, once more under the guidance of Rafa Benítez, entered the 2018/19 season with genuine optimism that another decent season could be on the cards. It was a tough start for United though as when the fixtures were released in June, the Magpies found four of last season's top six in their first five matches of the season. As it happens United lost all four by the odd goal but good performances counted for nothing in the points table and in the early days on the campaign, Rafa found his side in the relegation places. Results picked up and even though United rose no higher than 13th in the table, there were a number of stand out performances in the second half of the season, notably the win over eventual champions Manchester City. Indeed United were the last team to take any points off City before they went on a 14-game winning run to pip Liverpool to the title by one point.

AUGUST

The Magpies had an 'early' start to the season after being selected for the 12.30 kick off on Sky Sports on Saturday lunchtime. And incredibly the fixture computer churned out the identical fixture to the previous season, a home match-up with Tottenham Hotspur. Joselu had the honour of scoring United's first goal of the season but strikes from Jan Vertonghen and Dele Alli gave the Cockerels maximum points. A week later United should have returned from South Wales with all three points but had to settle for a 0-0 draw with Cardiff City after Kenedy missed from the penalty spot deep into injury time. Chelsea were on Tyneside for the last league fixture in August and for the third game in a row, the Sky cameras were on hand to catch the action. The deadlock wasn't broken until 15 minutes from time when Eden Hazard scored from the spot but when Joselu equalised with only seven minutes left, it looked like a good point had been earned by United. But in a late and unfortunate twist, DeAndre Yedlin put through his own goal to maintain the Blues' 100% start to the season. August also saw United bow out of the League Cup at the first hurdle, losing 3-1 at Nottingham Forest, even though the score two minutes into injury time was 1-1!

SEPTEMBER

It didn't get any easier with a trip to the Etihad next up and when DeAndre Yedlin equalised Raheem Sterling's early strike, it looked like an early season shock was on the cards. Sadly Kyle Walker rifled in a second half winner and unfortunately it was a case of a good performance not bringing any points. After the first international break of the season, another big gun in Arsenal were the next visitors at St. James' Park and like their North London rivals five weeks earlier, they took the three points back down south with them. A nil-nil draw at Selhurst Park earned United their second point of the season before the month ended in yet more disappointment as Leicester ran out 2 – 0 winners at St. James' Park with United conceding their second home penalty of the season. This had been a match United and their fans had targeted at least one point from hence the mood at the end of the month being somewhat downbeat with only two points on the board and only Cardiff and Fulham below them in the table. Indeed three of the bottom four in the table after only seven games ended up getting relegated, thankfully the Magpies were the odd ones out but it just goes to show how important a good start to the season is.

OCTOBER

Old Trafford was the first port of call in October and incredibly the Magpies opened up a two-goal lead in the opening 10 minutes through Kenedy and Yoshinori Mutō. And with 20 minutes left it was still 2-0 to the visitors with hopes of a second away win at the home of the Red Devils in five seasons becoming more than just a fanciful hope. Those dreams were shattered though as Jose Mourinho's men scored three times in the closing minutes including a last minute winner from Alexis Sanchez, the Chilean's only Premier League goal of the season! United hit rock-bottom two weeks later, following the second international break of the season, as after losing 1 – 0 to Brighton at St. James' Park, they sank to the bottom of the Premier League – thankfully that would be the only time that would happen all season. The month ended with a stalemate at Southampton meaning that all three points the Magpies had gained had been from away 0 -0 draws. The only way was up!

NOVEMBER

If United were going to make any progress up the Premier League now was the time. Successive home games against mid-table Watford and Bournemouth loomed large with, realistically, six points being the only option. And six points it was! Firstly an Ayoze Pérez header on 65 minutes from a perfectly delivered Ki free kick saw off the Hornets and seven days later it was a Salomón Rondón brace that proved too much for the Cherries. The game against Bournemouth also marked 100 years since the armistice with the club unveiling a grand new display in their memorial garden in the Milburn Stand, remembering all those United personnel who gave their lives for the country. And United made it three wins on the spin in their next fixture, their first Monday night Sky fixture of the season. Turf Moor, Burnley, was the venue and after Ben Mee put through his own net after only four minutes, Ciaran Clark doubled United's advantage 20 minutes later to seemingly put United in total control. A Sam Vokes strike just before half time changed the momentum and in the end United were just happy, and relieved, to be heading back to Tyneside with maximum points, not just on the night but from the month of November – an achievement that would earn Rafa Benitez the Manager of the Month award. For the record Benitez was the fourth United manager in the Premier League era to win the award, following in the footsteps of Messrs Keegan, Robson and Pardew.

DECEMBER

United only played three Premier League games in November but entered the festive period of December looking forward to seven games! The month got off to the worst possible start with United suffering their heaviest home defeat of the season, losing 3 - 0 to West Ham but United picked themselves off the floor four days later by picking up a deserved point at Goodison Park, Salomón Rondón scoring his third league goal of the season. It was back to St. James' Park the following weekend where the Magpies suffered injury time heartbreak when they rather sloppily allowed Wolves to claim a 94th minute winner – and that really hurt hard. Next up were third bottom Huddersfield and with United going into the game at the John Smith's Stadium only three points above the drop zone, this was a classic 'six-pointer'. And it was that man Rondón who finished off a fine flowing move to earn United a precious three points. Rafa was particularly disappointed that his side were unable to breach the leaky Fulham rear-guard at Gallowgate three days before Christmas, allowing the Cottagers to pick up only their second away point of the season. Boxing Day took United to Anfield and United endured a miserable day slipping to their only four-goal defeat of the season – a harsh penalty decision just after half-time possible contributing to their downfall before the month ended on a brighter note with a 1-1 draw at Watford to see the year out.

JANUARY

There was a huge game to bring in the New Year but disappointingly for the Geordies, the United of Manchester beat the United of Newcastle 2 - 0 on Tyneside. Three days later United drew their FA Cup Third Round tie with Blackburn 1 - 1 at St. James' Park but, possibly against the odds, won the replay 4 - 2 at Ewood Park with two players, Sean Longstaff and Callum Roberts, scoring their maiden United goals. In between the cup ties United lost 2-1 at Chelsea which was another case of performing well against a 'top-six' club but gaining no tangible reward. The Magpies hadn't won at home since 10 November so the visit of Cardiff was another of those clichéd 'must win' games. United didn't disappoint and their 3 - 0 win was thoroughly deserved and one of their most impressive and emphatic wins of the season. The FA Cup was back on the agenda the week after but in a competition much loved by the fans, United's dismal record in the cup over the past 15 years continued and they bowed out , 2 - 0, to eventual finalists Watford at St. James' Park. With United sat in 16th place in the table the

month drew to a close with the midweek visit of Champions Manchester City. The long odds on United winning would have lengthened after Sergio Aguero opened the scoring after a mind-boggling 24 seconds, and most neutrals would have expected the floodgates to open. This was a different, more resilient, United and they stood toe to toe with Pep Guardiola's side before forcing an equaliser just after the hour. And when Sean Longstaff was brought down in the box by Fernandinho and Matt Ritchie fired in the resultant penalty with ten minutes remaining, the roof lifted off at St. James' Park – what a night.

FEBRUARY

Wembley Stadium was United's first destination in February, sadly not for a Cup Final, but to play Tottenham in their temporary home as the rebuilding of White Hart Lane dragged on. In a dour contest, the Magpies looked set for a point until Son Heung-min popped up with a late winner. A week later, on Sky's Monday Night Football, against surprise package Wolves, United were denied victory at the death when a hotly disputed Willy Boly goal drew the home side level. Gut-wrenching but United now had two home games in the space of four days where six points would be the perfect cure for their Molineux hangover. First up were Huddersfield Town, 14 points from safety and virtually doomed, so a 2 – 0 home win was nothing less than expected. Burnley followed on the Tuesday evening and in repeating the 2-0 scoreline from the weekend, in a match that included a stunning Fabian Schär strike that won the BBC and Premier League Goal of the Month awards, United leap-frogged their Lancashire rivals in the table to move onto 31 points – that 'magic' figure of 40 now well within their sights.

MARCH

With another international break, never sure whether they come at good or bad times, March brought just three fixtures for Rafa Benitez to negotiate and in the end, a win, a draw and a defeat wasn't too bad an outcome, considering that it could easily have been three losses! First up was a trip to the London Stadium where West Ham's form had been a bit indifferent but the visiting United players probably put in one of their most low-key performances of the season in slumping to a 2 – 0 defeat. Local boy Sean Longstaff, who had been so impressive in his break-through season, also picked up a knee injury that would sadly rule him out for the remainder of the season. The following week the half time score at St. James' Park read Newcastle 0, Everton 2. Not looking great especially as Everton should have been down to ten-men. But roll on five to five and it read Newcastle 3, Everton 2! United had staged a stupendous comeback and with goals from Salomón Rondón and Ayoze Pérez (2) they turned the tide to record a remarkable victory at a pivotal time of the season. A week on and going into injury time at Bournemouth, the Magpies were 2 - 1 down and about to fall six points behind the Cherries. But then former home favourite Matt Ritchie hit a 'worldie' past Artur Boruc and United escaped from the south coast with an extremely valuable point.

APRIL

April's fixtures began on April Fools' Day and it was the visitors, Newcastle United, who were the fall guys, losing in lacklustre fashion to Arsenal at the Emirates. When a second consecutive defeat, also without scoring, followed at home to Crystal Palace, the alarm bells, although not ringing loudly, were just jangling a tiny bit with United's points total of 35 not quite being enough to enable everyone to relax. Leicester away, with the Foxes under the recently appointed Brendan Rodgers, looked tough on paper but as they did in 2017/18, they earned a fully-merited win at the King Power to move onto 38 points, still not quite there but edging a whole lot closer. And it was Ayoze Pérez, who had scored one of the two goals the previous season, who headed the only goal of the game – and what joy it brought to the travelling fans who stayed in the stadium for a good half hour after the final whistle serenading their heroes. And when Southampton were put to the sword the next weekend, with goal-machine Pérez hitting his first hat-trick in a black and white shirt, United cruised past the mythical 40-point mark. Brighton, still needing a point or two themselves, ended the month for United and the 1 - 1 draw played out at the Amex was probably a decent result for both sides.

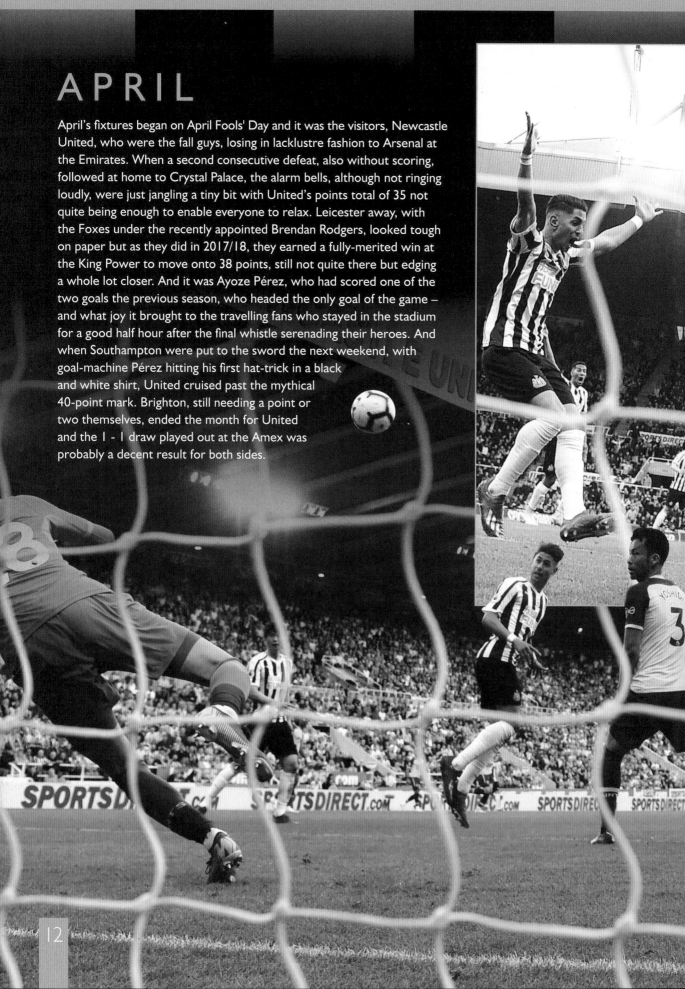

MAY

Two games to play and United had a part to play in the final destination of the Premier League title. Sandwiched in-between their Champions League semi-final ties with Barcelona, Liverpool came north to St. James' Park for a Saturday evening 7.45pm kick off – the first time United had played a league game at that time on a Saturday. With Manchester City not playing until the Monday night, the Reds knew a win would put them top of the table again whereas a draw or loss would be a dagger to the heart for their title hopes. At an atmospheric Gallowgate, with the noise booming around all four corners of the ground, it was the title-chasing visitors who led at the interval, but only by a slender 2 – 1 margin. Tyneside rocked with joy when Salomón Rondón netted a deserved equaliser ten minutes into the second half and with the sides trading blows as the game moved to its denouement, it was Jurgen Klopp's side who grabbed the winner, Divock Origi heading past Martin Dúbravka but only following the award of a debateable free-kick. United wrapped up the season with an easy four-goal romp at Craven Cottage, the game possibly being best remembered for around 1500 Newcastle supporters making their way to the ground by boat up the Thames!

The path to what will hopefully be a successful career in professional football more often than not begins at the Academy, unless you're someone like Jamie Vardy who came into the game at a later age from non-league football. Here, we take a look at life in the Academy with Year 3 scholar and Newcastle born goalkeeper Dan Langley.

A pupil at St Benet Biscop Catholic High School in Bedlington, Dan played for four renowned Boys Clubs; Blyth Town, Cramlington, Whitley Bay and Monkseaton before being awarded his scholarship in the autumn of 2017.

"Being part of the Academy set-up is a real privilege and something myself and all the lads are very proud of. We realise we're very fortunate to have been given this opportunity and that the hard work really starts here. Of course, there's no guarantee that you'll make it into the professional ranks, we all know that, but you've only got one chance in life and I can tell you, we're all giving it everything we've got. In this article I'm delighted to take you through a normal week of Academy life."

MONDAY

"We're all in for breakfast at around 8.30 and of course it's not a fry-up! We all eat very healthily and take in the nutrients we need for a tough morning ahead. Cereal, fruit, eggs, that sort of thing, plus plenty of liquids so we're always well hydrated.

"We start the day with one of our regular education sessions where we follow a BTEC Level 3 Diploma in Sport (Performance & Excellence) as well as an NVQ in Sporting Excellence. Our educational studies complement our football as we follow such units as sports psychology, nutrition and anatomy and physiology. We also look at current issues such as drugs in sport and health and safety. During our education sessions our tutors have also taken us into local schools to support the children with their reading and then to coach them football. This has been really enjoyable and helped me to develop my communication skills. We also do a lot of self-analysis of our own performances and look at areas that we need to develop within the four corners to progress as players. I personally chose to do several additional units in my second year scholarship and gained the Extended Diploma qualification. I feel that this is important as it gives me something to fall back on in the future. It also makes you into a better-rounded individual. I suppose you could call it 'life skills', and whilst we'd love it to be football 24/7, we all appreciate and understand the necessity to spend time in the classroom.

"We're then out on the training pitch soon after 10am and after the compulsory warm-up exercises, something it's very important to do, primarily to avoid injury when the serious training starts, we're into the specific goalkeeping drills be it handling, positioning, shot-stopping, crosses or commanding your penalty area. There's so many different aspects of goalkeeping we work on and hopefully, when it comes to the game, you can bring them altogether into one!

"We then join in with the outfield players for the rest of the session which is mainly game situation plays and we're done by about 12/12.30.

"Lunchtime is always a welcome break, a chance to refuel and also to relax a bit after the morning exertions. The chefs do a great job preparing the food; chicken, pasta, fish, vegetables, and plenty of it too which I need to fill my 6'6" frame!

"Finally for Monday, which is often the busiest day of the week, we look back and analyse the game we've just played the previous Saturday. Looking at the video, seeing what we've done right and how we could handle certain things better. Just watching yourself perform gives you a valuable insight into how you can improve."

TUESDAY

"A little bit like Monday but today we're in the gym straight after breakfast and we spend a good 45 minutes in there. Some of the lads have specific exercises they have to do but most of us have tailored programmes aimed at optimising our fitness so we can perform to our maximum potential.

"Training today is much the same Monday but in the goalkeeper sessions we're focussing on areas where the coaches think we need to strengthen. They leave no stone unturned and the advice and support we get is second to none.

"After lunch it's back to the gym which on Tuesdays is normally a gruelling weights session."

WEDNESDAY

"Ah Wednesdays. A full day of work with no football! Effectively this is 'education day' where we have two morning sessions and an afternoon session. This year we have followed a unit in sports psychology, we had to produce a project on what makes a successful team which we presented to the staff at the Academy. We also followed a unit called 'the athlete's lifestyle'. This was a really interesting unit as we looked at different factors that can impact upon the performances of professional athletes. The units give us an opportunity to look at other sports other than just football and also to spend time in the community (at local schools). These are all skills that help us to improve as players and individuals.

"It's actually good to have a day off football during the week, primarily just to give your body some rest and if you do have a little niggle, you can always pop in and see the physio for a bit of treatment ahead of training the next day."

THURSDAY

"Thursday's a bit like Tuesday in that we're in the gym first thing and focussing on power work. Then we train and after lunch we have a video analysis session which is team based and also looks ahead to the weekend's game. The technology we have in football today, and I'm sure in all sport, is mind-boggling at times compared to what it must have been like even 10 years ago but I have to say, from a personal point of view, it's an invaluable aid."

FRIDAY

"Friday begins with an education session before preparation starts for the match on Saturday. The training is specially focussed on how we're going to play the following day. Shape, tactics, set plays and all that sort of game specific stuff. Lunch and then off home to rest."

SATURDAY

"Matchday, at last, the best day of the week! Logistically if it's an away game and within easy reach, we're on the road at about 8am and have our pre-match meal on the bus but if it's a longer trip, say Birmingham or further, then it necessitates an overnight hotel stay. For home games, which normally kick-off at around 11am, we have to report by 9.30. We may look at some videos again, briefly, before we go out for the warm-up at around 10.10. Back in for 10.45/50, a last chat, focus and off we go!

SUNDAY

"A complete rest day and as far as I'm concerned if we've won the day before it's a good day, if we haven't, well it's not so good. I love my golf and if I can scramble a few holes (weather permitting) I'll do that otherwise I'll enjoy the football on TV and just look forward to starting over once again on Monday. I love it!"

"I hope you've enjoyed this look as life as a scholar in the Newcastle United Academy and if there's one bit of advice I can offer, it's to keep going, no matter what. My Grandad told me that if I kept believing with a determined and positive attitude, I'd get my chance, and he's been proved right."

With the World Cup having just been held in France, the profile of women's football is on a very much upward trend.

Newcastle United Women are an English women's football club, affiliated with Newcastle United FC.

The team was founded 30 years ago in 1989 and at the moment they train twice a week at the Newcastle United Academy Training Centre in Benton. Home matches are played at Druid Park in the Woolsington district of Newcastle.

Newcastle United are currently members of the FA Women's National League Division One North which is the fourth-level in the women's football league pyramid in England, along with Division One South. These two divisions are part of the FA Women's National League and sit below the FA Women's Super League, FA Women's Championship and Women's Northern Premier League.

In the summer of 2016, the Women's team became officially affiliated with Newcastle United FC, bringing the two clubs together and strengthening links between the women's club and the Newcastle United Foundation.

In the 2018/19 season the team, managed by Jill Stacey and Andy Inness, finished ninth in the League which was won by Burnley FC Women. Season highlights included a derby away win against local rivals Chester-le-Street Ladies and Norton & Stockton, with both games finishing 1-0 to the black and whites. The team also progressed to the first round of the SSE Women's FA Cup with an Abbie Joice free kick that secured a 3-2 extra time win away at league rivals Barnsley.

It's well known that Salomón Rondón was named Newcastle United's Player of the Year for 2018/19 but less well known is that Grace Donnelly lifted the Women's equivalent award whilst Steph Ord won the Golden Boot for being top goalscorer. Meanwhile the Young Player of the Year award went to Jayden Maxwell.

Grace

Steph

Jayden

Speaking on behalf of the team, captain Brooke Cochrane said:

Brooke

"All the girls are immensely proud each week to pull on the famous black and white jersey and represent Newcastle United.

"We all love playing football and to be able to do so for your local team is a tremendous feeling each week. We're fans after all and we take great pride in our approach to the game.

"Obviously we're not professionals like the men but our commitment and dedication to training and playing is second to none and we play to win, aside from enjoying every minute of it as well.

"We have a huge passion to achieve success and this season (2019/20) our aim has to be promotion to the Northern Premier League. Last season it was disappointing to finish only ninth in the National League but we all have a belief we can kick on and improve not just as individuals but as a club too."

For further details on the Women's team please email Lisa Bell at the Newcastle United Foundation. (lisa.bell@nufc.co.uk)

17

What is a cult hero in football? The definition is not something that is set in stone but is probably best summed up as 'one who has achieved hero status for perhaps unconventional reasons but isn't necessarily successful and is maybe greatly admired by a relatively small audience.' Furthermore, somewhat contradictory, a cult hero is not supposed to be the best, though they might just have been!

Albert Shepherd (1908-1914)

123 appearances, 92 goals

A centre-forward who left his mark on United's history books in spectacular fashion. Shepherd lead the line with lightning pace and also scored on his England debut. Following his big transfer to United, and remember the Geordies were the best team in the land back in the 1900s, Albert quickly became a crowd hero; that despite making his home debut in the infamous 9-1 derby defeat by Sunderland! United did win the title that season though. Such was his confidence in front of goal that he once asked United's directors if he could leave a game early provided he scored a hat-trick – which he duly did. Shepherd netted twice during the 1910 FA Cup final win over Barnsley, including the first penalty in a cup final. After his career finished Albert worked in his native Lancashire mills before becoming a well-known landlord at the Crown & Cushion public house in Bolton.

Hatem Ben Arfa (2010- 2015)

88 appearances, 14 goals

Magical and maddening, entertaining and enigmatic, Hatem was an immensely talented striker/midfielder player, the type of player that when he got the ball, the crowd held their breath in anticipation for what would happen next. Signing from Marseille, Hatem debuted as a substitute at home to Blackpool in September 2010 and got off the mark in spectacular style with the winning goal at Everton a week later. He suffered a horrific double leg break at Manchester City a few weeks later, recovering to score one of the best goals seen on Tyneside in the FA Cup tie with Blackburn in January 2012, then his opener against Bolton that April, a stunning solo effort from his own half, was another classic strike. Sometimes hugely frustrating, but a genuine cult hero.

Tino Asprilla (1996-1998)

63 appearances, 18 goals

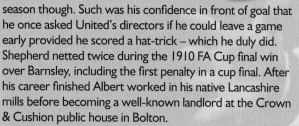

The record £7.5m signing of Asprilla was surrounded in controversy and, at times, media hysteria. The transfer from Parma was a long, drawn out affair but when he arrived on Tyneside he proved to be flamboyant, hugely talented and a one-off special player. A unique entertainer, he hit the headlines on the pitch for his brilliant and outlandish performances, witness his hat-trick against Barcelona, but equally was in the limelight off the pitch too but, that said, much of the hype that followed him was exaggerated. Debuting at Middlesbrough where he created United's equaliser with an incredible 'drag-back' and cross, Tino was loved by the Geordies and left an indelible stamp on English football when he departed after two seasons at St. James' Park.

Alan Foggon (1965-71)

80 appearances, 16 goals

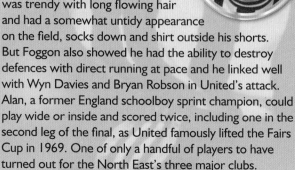

Alan Foggon joined United as a junior from West Stanley in 1965 and two years later signed professionally with the Magpies before the start of the 1967/68 season, making his debut as a 17-year-old at Arsenal. The teenager was a happy-go-lucky kid when he burst onto the scene, perhaps characterising the era, he was trendy with long flowing hair and had a somewhat untidy appearance on the field, socks down and shirt outside his shorts. But Foggon also showed he had the ability to destroy defences with direct running at pace and he linked well with Wyn Davies and Bryan Robson in United's attack. Alan, a former England schoolboy sprint champion, could play wide or inside and scored twice, including one in the second leg of the final, as United famously lifted the Fairs Cup in 1969. One of only a handful of players to have turned out for the North East's three major clubs.

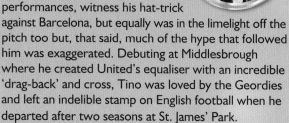

So a cult figure is not necessarily one of United's famous heroes, like an Alan Shearer or Malcolm Macdonald, but one who did have a cult following and, more importantly still does. Here we list, alphabetically, a selection of players who most fans will accept achieved cult status at St. James' Park.

Ray 'Rocky' Hudson (1971-1978)

29 appearances, 2 goals

Rocky Hudson a born and bred Tynesider from Dunston, who spoke with the broadest Geordie accept you can imagine, was a hugely talented ball-playing midfielder who first appeared in the Magpies line-up as an 18-year-old. In his brief time at Gallowgate, he wowed many a young fan with his trickery and flamboyant style of play but four years on from making his debut, and finding it tough to cement a permanent place in the United midfield, he moved to the glamour world of the United States and the Fort Lauderdale Strikers where he found the perfect stage to show off and showcase his skills in the Florida sunshine. Playing alongside international stars such as George Best and Gerd Muller, Ray enjoyed the best years of his career, sadly for those Geordie fans who hugely admired him, it was over 4,000 miles away!

Temuri Ketsbaia (1997-2000)

109 appearances, 14 goals

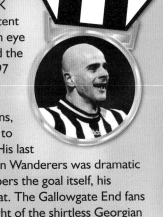

The Georgian, nicknamed the 'mad monk' by United supporters, joined the Magpies from AEK Athens. Sometimes inconsistent and unpredictable, he had an eye for goal and famously scored the goal in Zagreb in August 1997 that sent United into the Champions League group stages. Eccentric on occasions, Ketsbaia took his inner rage to a whole new level in 1998. His last minute winner against Bolton Wanderers was dramatic enough but no-one remembers the goal itself, his celebration made sure of that. The Gallowgate End fans were then treated to the sight of the shirtless Georgian kicking and mutilating the St James' Park advertising hoardings in what remains arguably the most infamous celebration in Premier League history. It brought him cult status at Newcastle United!

Bill McCracken (1904-1923)

444 appearances, 8 goals

United have had some colourful full-backs over the years but, without question, one of the most influential was Belfast-born Bill McCracken. Such was his grasp of the offside trap, the often controversial defender forced football's authorities into a tactical rethink and a change of the rules in 1925. Much loved on Tyneside, but the target of abuse on away grounds, McCracken was also often in dispute with the game's authorities as he enjoyed an exuberant lifestyle marked by a mischievous sense of humour. Having arrived at the club as a second-choice right-back, the Irish international went on to make the position his own, spending an amazing 19 years as a Newcastle player. Much revered by those who saw him play.

Ron McGarry (1962-67)

132 appearances, 46 goals

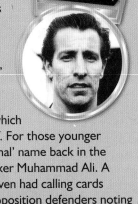

Ron was a tough bustling striker who could play the number nine role or both inside forward positions. He took punishment from defenders but was always able to dish out a fair share of retribution, both in terms of goals and physical retaliation, hence his nickname of 'Cassius' which he picked up after an infamous altercation with Swansea's Mike Johnson and which saw the United striker sent-off. For those younger readers, Cassius was the 'original' name back in the 1960s of the world famous boxer Muhammad Ali. A laugh-a-minute character, he even had calling cards printed which he handed to opposition defenders noting 'Have Goals Will Travel'. Today he retains his witty personality and still has a legion of fans on Tyneside.

Mirandinha (1987-1990)

67 appearances 24 goals

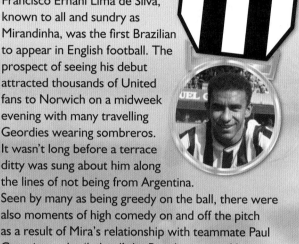

Francisco Ernani Lima de Silva, known to all and sundry as Mirandinha, was the first Brazilian to appear in English football. The prospect of seeing his debut attracted thousands of United fans to Norwich on a midweek evening with many travelling Geordies wearing sombreros. It wasn't long before a terrace ditty was sung about him along the lines of not being from Argentina.

Seen by many as being greedy on the ball, there were also moments of high comedy on and off the pitch as a result of Mira's relationship with teammate Paul Gascoigne who 'helped' the Brazilian expand his English vocabulary. Famously, after a home defeat to Wimbledon in 1989, he crept up behind Wombles 'keeper Dave Beasant and kicked him up the rear before running off. And then there was Mira's pig farm but we won't go down that avenue!

John McNamee (1966-1971)

132 appearances, 8 goals

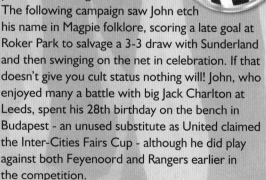

A tough no-nonsense centre half who rebuffed an approach from Matt Busby to move to Manchester United in 1958 when he worked in the Glasgow shipyards. Joining the Magpies in December 1966, after four dismissals had made him something of a marked man in Scotland, his performances helped United pull clear of relegation that season. The following campaign saw John etch his name in Magpie folklore, scoring a late goal at Roker Park to salvage a 3-3 draw with Sunderland and then swinging on the net in celebration. If that doesn't give you cult status nothing will! John, who enjoyed many a battle with big Jack Charlton at Leeds, spent his 28th birthday on the bench in Budapest - an unused substitute as United claimed the Inter-Cities Fairs Cup - although he did play against both Feyenoord and Rangers earlier in the competition.

Jimmy Smith (1969-76)

178 appearances, 16 goals

'Jinky' Jimmy Smith was an outstanding ball player who was United's first six-figure incoming transfer when he moved from Aberdeen to Tyneside. A master craftsman, Jinky could send the crowd into raptures when 'in the mood'. He had a languid, lazy style and possessed a tantalising right foot featuring the piece de resistance – the Jinky 'nutmeg' which quickly became the talk of Tyneside. Hampered by knee injuries, he was good enough to win International honours for Scotland. Once sent-off after only 53 seconds against Birmingham, his magical performances mean he will always be remembered as one of United's finest and a hero to a generation of United supporters.

Albert Stubbins (1936-1946)

217 appearances, 237 goals

Wallsend born, Albert was a legend in football, firstly for his amazing goalscoring exploits during the second world war years and afterwards, for being featured on the cover of the Beatles' Sergeant Pepper's Lonely Hearts Club Band, as a Merseyside icon. Tall and leggy, Stubbins had a terrific turn of pace and loved to run at defenders, he packed a ferocious shot and during the war smashed goals from every angle. He was the country's best striker, a real personality, hitting an incredible 230 goals in seven seasons of war time football. Nicknamed the 'Smiling Assassin' he was a gentleman of the game. Revered on Tyneside, with cult status, he also found success at Liverpool before becoming a respected journalist back in Newcastle.

Other players, possibly worthy of a mention as cult heroes would include, Martin Burleigh, Franz Carr, Daniel Cordone, Howard Gayle, Paul Goddard, Aleksandar Mitrovic, Andy O'Brien, Mick Quinn, Kenny Wharton (for sitting on the ball) and Billy Whitehurst. And maybe there's one or two we haven't mentioned that you would include!

QUIZ ONE

What do you remember about United last season?

? Who scored United's penultimate goal of last season?

? Against which team did Miguel Almirón make his debut?

? Who was the only United player to start every league game last season?

? Which two Newcastle players were red carded last season?

? Which three teams didn't score against United at home and away?

? In home and away games which team scored the most goals against United?

? Who did United record their lowest home league attendance against?

? Who played only four minutes of league football last season?

? Who did United play at home in their only pre-season friendly?

? In which away game did United play in their change strip for the first time?

QUIZ TWO

And how's your knowledge about Newcastle United in the Premier League era?

? Which is the only team United scored seven against?

? Who is United's second top scorer behind Alan Shearer?

? United have only scored five away from home once, against whom?

PLAYER Q&A

FEDERICO FERNANDEZ

Boyhood Hero?
Roberto Ayala (Argentine defender 1991-2011)

Best Footballing Moment?
Can I have three? My first game for Estudiantes in 2008, scoring twice on my Champions League debut and playing in the 2014 World Cup for Argentina.

Toughest Opponent?
Diego Costa

Team Supported As A Boy?
River Plate

Pre-Match Meal?
Pasta & Chicken

Any Superstitions?
Always have a coffee before the game in the same place!

Favourite Current Player?
Lionel Messi

Favourite Other Sports Person?
Tiger Woods and Rafa Nadal

Favourite Stadium Other Than St. James' Park?
I have three again! Bayern Munich, Liverpool and Boca Juniors

What Would You be If You Weren't A Footballer?
A PE Teacher

Where Did You Go For Your 2019 Summer Holiday?
Argentina, Miami, Turks & Caicos and the Bahamas

What Do You Like In Particular About The City Of Newcastle?
Walking around the city centre, the architecture and the bridges over the Tyne

Favourite Actor?
Adam Sandler

Favourite Music Artist / Last Concert Seen?
Ricardo Arjona (Latin-American singer songwriter)

What Do You Like Doing In Your Spare Time?
Being with my family

Best Friend In Football?
Érik Lamela (my Argentine compatriot at Tottenham)

Which Three People Would You Invite Round For Dinner?
Lionel Messi, Diego Maradona and Gabriel Batistuta

Which Boots Do You Wear?
Adidas Predator

What's The Best Goal You've Scored?
For Napoli against Bayern Munich

Favourite PS4 / Xbox Game?
I'm one of the few who doesn't play

KI SUNGYUENG

Boyhood Hero?
Zinedine Zidane

Best Footballing Moment?
Winning the bronze medal at the 2012 Olympics. We [South Korea] beat Japan 2-0 in the bronze medal match in Cardiff.

Toughest Opponent?
The Man City team at the Etihad in the 2017/18 season. They beat us [Swansea] 5-0.

Team Supported As A Boy?
Arsenal

Pre-Match Meal?
Bread and fish

Any Superstitions?
I don't have any. I believe in God

Favourite Current Player?
Frenkie de Jong (Barcelona)

Favourite Other Sports Person?
Steph Curry (Golden State Warriors)

Favourite Stadium Other Than St. James' Park?
Anfield

What Would You Be If You Weren't A Footballer?
Probably a teacher

Where Did You Go For Your 2019 Summer Holiday?
I spent time back home in South Korea

What Do You Like In Particular About The City Of Newcastle?
The passion of the fans

Favourite Actor?
Denzel Washington

Favourite Music Artist / Last Concert Seen?
I haven't seen them, but I like Maroon 5

What Do You Like Doing In Your Spare Time?
Playing with my daughter (aged 4)

Best Friend In Football?
Lee Chung-yong who plays for Bochum in Germany

Which Three People Would You Invite Round For Dinner?
Lionel Messi, my late Grandmother and Maroon 5

Which Boots Do You Wear?
Nike Magista or Vapor

What's The Best Goal You've Scored?
The goal I scored for Celtic against Motherwell in the 2011 Scottish Cup Final

Favourite PS4 / Xbox Game?
I play a few games on my PS4

SPOT THE BALL

Can you spot the ball in this match last season between Newcastle and Southampton?

And what about in this match against Tottenham?

Answers can be found on page 62.

The format, size and, of course, price of the matchday programme, a bible for many fans who attend matches at St. James' Park, has changed considerably down the years. In this feature, we look back at 60 years of Newcastle United programmes – essential reading for young and old.

1990-91

1991-92

1992-93

1993-94

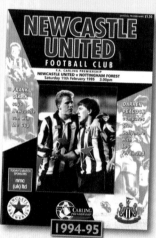

1994-95

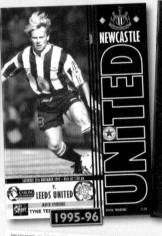

1995-96

1996-97

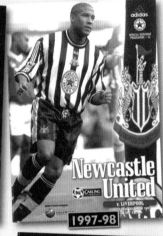

1997-98

1998-99

1999-2000

2000-01

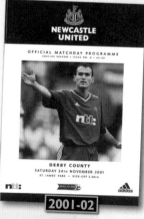

2001-02

2002-03

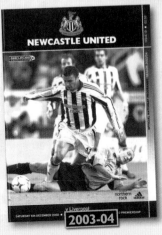

2003-04

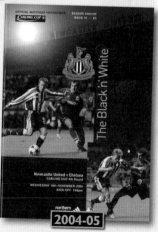

2004-05

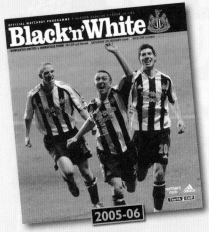

2005-06

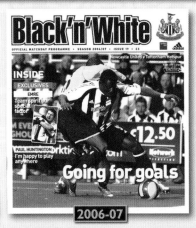

2006-07

2007-08

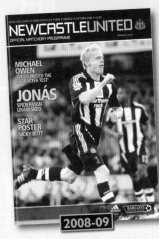

2008-09

2009-10

2010-11

2011-12

2012-13

2013-14

2014-15

2015-16

2016-17

2017-18

2018-19

2019-20

SEAN LONGSTAFF

This is a story about a local boy made good, one who has risen right through the academy ranks to first-team football – and that's a journey every budding North East footballer dreams about.

Sean, like Paul Dummett before him, has shown that's possible and their passage from the school playing fields of Tyneside to walking out on the pristine turf at such venues as Wembley Stadium and Anfield, is real 'boys own' stuff.

Born in North Shields 22 years ago, Sean joined the United set up as a nine-year-old in 2007 and signed scholarship forms in July 2014.

He'd actually made his Under 18 debut the previous season against Arsenal as a 16-year-old but the 2014/15 season proved to be his breakthrough year, making 30 appearances for United and chipping in with a fantastic tally of 15 goals from his attacking midfield position.

Although Sean made his first team debut at Nottingham Forest in a League Cup tie in August 2018, it wasn't until Boxing Day that Sean's Premier League dreams were realised when he came on against Liverpool as a 73rd minute substitute. And with former Koppite Steven Gerrard being his favourite player as a youngster, it was kind of appropriate Anfield was the setting for what Sean, his family and United fans all around the country will hope was just the start of a successful career as a professional footballer.

"I'd been on the bench for a few games but when the gaffer said I was going on for Kenedy with about 15 minutes left it was unbelievable. It's every young lad's dream in Newcastle to run on and hear the fans chanting. It's a great feeling and it's something you want to try and do over and over again. It gives you the incentive to push on and make yourself a regular. It was an unbelievable day, especially with my family in the crowd behind the goal, I was just over the moon to make my Premier League debut."

Life changed beyond all recognition in the space of a few months last year for Sean but

"I haven't changed", he said. "I'm still the same humble lad who lives at home with my family."

But back to the beginning. "I've been playing football for as long as I can remember", Sean recalls, "Probably from around two or three years old and coming from a sporting family (his Dad is a former Great Britain Ice Hockey player), it was just a natural thing to do. Dad was great, he saw we were better at football (as opposed to ice hockey) and pushed us towards that - it was the right decision!

"I remember playing for Astley Under 6s and back then I played all over the place, but mainly as a striker, as I did at school. I also played a bit with North Shields and Cramlington before joining the United set-up which, looking back, was the first step in my aim to make it as a footballer.

"Back then of course I had no idea how my future would unravel but even in the early days I knew I was fortunate to have been given this opportunity and there was only was person who could work to make the dream come true, and that was me!

"That said, there's no way I would have got anywhere near the first team if it hadn't been for the support of my family and the various age-level coaches at Newcastle United who I owe a huge debt of gratitude to.

"It was non-stop football and I loved every minute of it. I'd play for Longbenton on Saturdays then Newcastle United on Sundays, for the Under 10s, Under 11s and Under 12s but when I got to 13 or 14 it was just Newcastle I played for with the games being on Saturday mornings.

"From the Under 16s the next progression was to the Under 18s and during the 2014/15 season I was lucky enough to get my chance with the Under 21s and actually got a hat-trick on my debut in a Northumberland Senior Cup tie. It was unreal!

First team debut

U11s

U12s

SEAN LONGSTAFF

"At that time, just as I was turning 18, I wasn't sure about getting a professional contract but that just made me even more determined to succeed. I knew I had the ability to make it, but I had to convince other people to share that view too. That's where the support of my family was so important. They believed in me and were 100 per cent behind me so when I went off to Kilmarnock on loan in the second half of the 2016/17 season, I knew it was something that could be the making of me.

"The following season, in August 2017, I went to Blackpool where I scored my first football league goal and there's no doubt without those loan spells there was probably no way I was going to be able to come back into the first team environment at Newcastle and be as comfortable as I was. I'm really lucky that I had that, and the people at both clubs were absolutely brilliant with me. I cannot thank them enough for giving me the opportunity to start my professional career. It toughened me up, took me out of my comfort zone (i.e. being at home) and above all else, proved to myself that I could mix it in the professional ranks.

"A year on and I got a chance in the pre-season games and even scored in the game over in Ireland against St. Patrick's. From then on though it was a case of just keeping my head down, working as hard as I possibly could and just waiting for an opportunity. Of course the icing on the cake was the Liverpool game, but a few weeks before that I signed a new three and a half year contract with the club which was, my Dad said, due reward for the incredible amount of hard graft I'd put in over the years to achieve my goal.

"I'm still learning every day, last season was brilliant for me and it gave me a lot of confidence to think I can go in and play against the top players and best teams in the Premier League. In the past 12 months I think I've improved loads as a player, and as a person too which is important, and just playing in those games after Christmas helped me massively.

"We needed some wins to get away from the wrong end of the table, which we did, and just helping the team to pick up a few results here and there was an amazing feeling. [Longstaff is too modest to admit how scoring against Burnley in February was a personal career high for him and helped earn the three points that night… but that's just typical of a lad who is the perfect role model for any aspiring youngster].

"So that's the journey so far and my message to any young lad who wants to become a professional footballer is to remember talent on its own isn't enough. Put in the hard work and be as dedicated to the profession as you can but whilst that's never an absolute guarantee to success, it'll give you a chance and you can't ask for any more than that."

U15s

U18s

New contract

First Premier League goal

Premier League debut

29

A lovely picture of some of the 1951 FA Cup winning team, relaxing away from the pitch. United beat Blackpool 2-0 in the Final at Wembley and went on to win the Cup in 1952 and 1955 as well, the Cup kings of the 50s! Amongst those pictured are centre-half Frank Brennan (front row third left) and captain Joe Harvey on Frank's left.

Stand in captain Frank Clark shakes hands with West Ham skipper Bobby Moore before the First Division fixture at St. James' Park on 10 August 1968. The match finished 1-1 with Bryan 'Pop' Robson scoring for United and Brian Dear equalising for the Hammers in the last minute. Moore of course had captained England to World Cup glory two years earlier.

March 1974 and United are on their way to Wembley. Tommy Cassidy (left) and Jimmy Smith (right) are amongst those congratulating goalscorer Malcolm Macdonald as his brace in the semi-final at Hillsborough was enough to send the Magpies to the FA Cup Final. A forlorn Burnley keeper Alan Stevenson looks on as United fans in all parts of the ground celebrate.

Manager Joe Harvey looks on from the dug-out area in the old West Stand (now Milburn Stand) as John Tudor, Frank Clark and Malcolm Macdonald are put through their paces at a training session at St. James' Park. The picture is from the 1971/72 season and you can just see the top of the old Leazes End roof in the top right hand corner.

Captain Jimmy Scoular, pictured on the left of the FA Cup, leads the team round the cinder track at St. James' Park as the 1955 FA Cup winners triumphantly return to Tyneside and show off the famous old trophy at a packed St. James' Park. The previous day United had beaten Manchester City 3-1 in the Final which had included a goal in just 45 seconds from Jackie Milburn.

Washing the team kit from the Edwardian era! Back in the 1900s the laundry facilities probably weren't quite what they are these days. No tumble dryers in sight, just a washing line and a good breeze to get the kit spic and span ready for the next game. And of course kits had to last a season back then, not a case of just grabbing a brand new one from the kit room 110 years ago.

The bottom entrance into St. James' Park in the 1960s. This picture is taken from Strawberry Place and looks up the hill towards the old West Stand. If you were standing in the same spot today it would be a completely different view with the Sir Bobby Robson statue on the right. You can also just see two of the old floodlight pylons peering over the West Stand.

May 1993 and United have just beaten Leicester City 7-1 at St. James' Park, it was 6-0 at half time! Andy Cole and David Kelly both scored hat-tricks. After the game United were presented with the Championship trophy and are seen here, led by manager Kevin Keegan, on their lap of honour. The players at the front of the group, left to right, are Rob Lee, Mark Robinson, Brian Kilcline and Alex Mathie. The Premier League awaited the re-born Magpies.

Back in 1972 the old Popular side of the ground was demolished to make way for a new stand, simply called the East Stand. Today it's the only surviving part of the ground from the mid-1970s. The East Stand opened to much acclaim in early 1973 with the Magpies having to play much of that season with a three-sided ground. The Gallowgate End terrace is in the background, with the scoreboard of course at the back.

It's 1948 and trainer Andy McCombie, still going strong aged 72, is seen here checking out and repairing the players' boots. No fancy stud spanners in those days, a hammer was all that was needed to nail the studs in place. And all the boots looked much the same too, no coloured light-weight boots 70 years ago. McCombie was a League Championship winner with United in his playing days at the club in the 1900s.

An A-Z with a difference this year, this time it's memorable matches going back some 120 years, including the Edwardian era when United were the best team in the country.

A IS FOR ARSENAL

The 4-4 draw with the Gunners back in February 2011. If you recall, United were 4-0 down at half time, and staring an absolute hammering in the face. But then they got one back, then another, a third duly arrived and then incredibly, with just three minutes remaining, Cheick Tioté smashed in a never-to-be-forgotten equaliser.

B IS FOR BARCELONA

United had qualified for the Champions League for the first time and their first group game was against the 1992 European Champions. On one of the greatest nights in United's history, they raced into a 3-0 lead, thanks to a sensational Tino Asprilla hat-trick before running out 3-2 winners.

C IS FOR CARLISLE UNITED

It's back to the 1983/84 promotion season and a fantastic Easter Monday fixture at St. James' Park against the Cumbrians. United were 2-0 up when the visitors were awarded a penalty. Former United striker Alan Shoulder saw his kick saved by Kevin Carr and United immediately broke upfield to make it 3-0. A real turning point in their eventual 5-1 win.

D IS FOR DONCASTER ROVERS

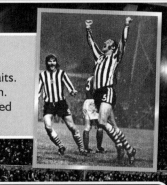

It's October 1973 and a low-key League Cup tie against Doncaster Rovers awaits. United are 5-0 up with 11 minutes left when the ground erupts to hail one man. Left back Frank Clark has just smashed in his first goal for the club and it's celebrated like a cup winning strike! Frank only scored twice for United in 487 appearances.

E IS FOR EVERTON

Back to November 1959 and, two days after Guy Fawkes night, there were more fireworks at St. James' Park where 10 goals were shared by the two clubs, luckily United scored eight of them! The Magpies scored four in each half with Len White helping himself to a hat-trick. Later in the season they also smashed seven past Manchester United.

F IS FOR FULHAM

Newcastle hold the record for the biggest winning margin in an FA Cup semi-final. Back in 1908, when United reached five Cup finals in six years either side of this fixture against the Cottagers, the Magpies hit Fulham for six but sadly couldn't take that form into the final, losing out 3-1 to Wolves.

G IS FOR GRIMSBY TOWN

On a memorable night in Cleethorpes in May 1993, goals from Andy Cole and David Kelly gave United a 2-0 win over the Mariners which clinched promotion to the Premier League for Kevin Keegan's side. United ended that record-breaking season (11 wins in a row at the start) with a 7-1 thrashing of Leicester City.

H IS FOR HEREFORD UNITED

This game is included for all the wrong reasons but it's still one of the most famous in United's history, and every time FA Cup third round weekend comes around, it's always a hot talking point. In a nutshell, the Southern League part-timers drew 2-2 at St. James' Park before incredibly winning the replay 2-1 at Edgar Street which included a one in a million 35-yard thunderbolt from Ronnie Radford.

I IS FOR INTER MILAN

Newcastle took over 10,000 supporters to the Italian fashion capital of Milan in March 2003 and came away with a 2-2 draw in a game they could well have won. Alan Shearer scored twice for United in the San Siro, a result that meant they went into their final game with Barcelona still with a chance of finishing in the top two in the group.

J IS FOR JUVENTUS

The only 'J' team we've played so an easy choice. And it has to be the 1-0 home win over the Italian giants back in October 2002. United had lost their first three group stage matches in the Champions League so this was a 'must-win' game. The Magpies obliged with a single goal from the unlikely right-boot of full-back Andy Griffin. And what's more United won their next two games to qualify for the next round!

K IS FOR KILMARNOCK

Newcastle United have never played a competitive match against a team beginning with K so we've had to dig up a friendly match with Kilmarnock from out of the archives from years gone by, 1903 infact. Suffice to say there's not a lot of detail available about the game other that United won 2-0 at Rugby Park with goals from Jack Carr (right) and Bill Appleyard.

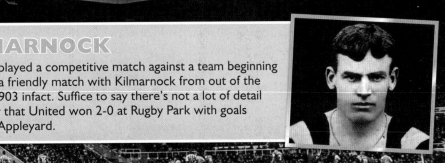

L IS FOR LILLESTRØM

When United played the Norwegian Eliteserien side on 15 July 2006, it set a record for the earliest competitive starting date to a season in United's 127 year history. It was an Intertoto Cup Third Round First Leg tie and a single Albert Luque goal settled the tie in favour of United who would go on to reach the last 16 of the UEFA Cup that season.

M IS FOR MARSEILLE

The side from southern France, who won the Champions League in 1993 (just after former United winger Chris Waddle had left them), were United's glamour opponents in the semi-finals of the UEFA Cup in April/May 2004. After an enthralling 0-0 draw at St. James' Park, two Didier Drogba goals sent Les Phocéens into the Final where they would be beaten by Valencia.

N IS FOR NEWPORT COUNTY

Well it had to be. On 5 October 1946 Newport County visited St. James' Park and returned to South Wales on the wrong end of a 13-0 scoreline – the highest margin of victory in the top two divisions of English league football. Len Shackleton scored six, Charlie Wayman four, Jackie Milburn two with Roy Bentley completing the scoring.

O IS FOR OLDHAM

One of the most enjoyable games in the early years of the Entertainers was the televised 3-1 win over Oldham in November 1993. Trailing at half time, United produced an outstanding second half display to turn the game on its head. Goals from Andy Cole (2) and Peter Beardsley did the trick for United. The same two players had shared the goals in the previous week's 4-0 win over Wimbledon.

P IS FOR PÉCSI DÓZSA

This Fairs Cup tie in October/November 1970 turned out to be United's last foray into Europe for seven years. Coasting after a comfortable 2-0 home first leg win, United travelled to Pécs, still on a high after their previous years exploits in the competition, but dismally lost the return leg 2-0 to the unfancied Hungarians. Inevitably they contrived to lose the penalty shoot-out 3-0 after missing their first three spot kicks.

Q IS FOR QUEENS PARK RANGERS

Another easy choice as they're the only Q United have played. There have been some great games down the years but none more remarkable than the 5-5 draw at Loftus Road back in September 1984. Amazingly United led 4-0 at half time, QPR clawed it back to 4-4, United went in front again before the hosts grabbed a last minute equaliser. In amongst the chaos there was a hat-trick for Chris Waddle.

R IS FOR ROTHERHAM UNITED

Shortly after Kevin Keegan sensationally joined United, the Magpies travelled to Millmoor for a Division Two clash with the Millers in October 1982. And in front of the BBC Match of the Day cameras, Keegan scored four in a magnificent 5-1 win for the Geordies. For the record Kevin Todd scored United's fifth.

S IS FOR SWINDON TOWN

Sunderland would have been too obvious so we've selected the Wiltshire outfit instead. Why? Well because before United famously smashed eight goals past Sheffield Wednesday in Bobby Robson's first home game to set their Premier League record winning score, United racked up a terrific 7-1 victory over the Robins in their first season back in the top flight, 1993/94.

T IS FOR TOW LAW TOWN

Yes, United have met the Durham village side in competitive matches. Both times were in the FA Cup, firstly in October 1891 and then again in December 1895. Not surprisingly the Magpies won both ties, 5-1 and 4-0. Centre forward Willie Thompson was the only United player to feature in both games.

U IS FOR ÚJPEST DÓZSA

Újpest are the only side beginning with U that the Magpies have met. And, of course, a very famous one as we've just passed the 50th anniversary of United beating the Hungarians 6-2 on aggregate to win the Inter-Cities Fairs Cup on their first excursion into Europe. Captain Bob Moncur remarkably scored a hat-trick over the course of the two-legged final.

V IS FOR VITÓRIA SETÚBAL

United have played three teams beginning with V, all in European encounters, but it's the games with Vitória Setúbal in the Fairs Cup back in March 1969 that stand out. In snowy conditions United won the first leg of the quarter final tie 5-1 at St. James' Park and despite losing the return leg 3-1 in Portugal, they progressed to the semi-finals.

W IS FOR WEST BROMWICH ALBION

United have met the Baggies on 128 occasions but no game stands out quite like the 1974 FA Cup Fifth Round tie at the Hawthorns. Wearing their 'Brazil' away strip the Magpies performed like the South American artisans in playing a superb brand of football to win 3-0 in-front of a huge travelling support who would eventually see United reach Wembley for the Cup Final.

X NO X FACTOR TEAMS...

So we're cheating a bit and going for Crewe Alexandra. Somewhat surprisingly the clubs have met on nine occasions but six of those were in Division Two back in the 1890s. Most memorably was the League Cup tie at Gresty Road in October 1991. Three down after 22 minutes United fought back to win 4-3 thanks mainly to a Gavin Peacock hat-trick.

Y IS FOR YORK CITY

Can you imagine little York City being in the FA Cup semi-finals. Well incredibly they progressed that far back in 1955 and came out of the hat against United. And it needed a replay for the Magpies to see off plucky City who at that time were a Football League Division Three North side. The Minstermen had reached that far in the competition for the first time in their history which had included a fifth-round victory over Tottenham.

Z IS FOR ŽELJEZNIČAR

The Bosnian side that United played in the Qualifying Round of the 2002/03 Champions League. Kieron Dyer scored the only goal of the game in the first leg in Sarajevo before the Magpies eased past their Balkan opponents 4-0 in the return at St. James' Park to comfortably take their place in a group containing Feyenoord, Juventus and Dynamo Kiev.

Newcastle United lifted the Inter-Cities Fairs Cup, the forerunner to the Europa League, in 1969 and, last April, four of that cup-winning squad returned to Budapest as guests of Újpest FC. The players involved were club captain Bob Moncur (who scored three goals in the two-legged final), Alan Foggon (who scored in the away leg in Hungary), John Craggs and Keith Dyson. Here is the pictorial story of their visit, as told by Bob.

Here are the lads at Newcastle Airport on the Friday morning (26 April) before our flight to Budapest. Left to right it's Keith Dyson, John Craggs, Alan Foggon and me. We flew British Airways to London and then on to Budapest.

This is the view across the river looking towards the Royal Palace. Some of the architecture around the city was a sight to behold and I was really pleased we had a chance to look around, something we weren't able to do when we came 50 years ago. We're pictured with Budapest resident Laszlo Nemeth, a former England team Basketball Coach who was our tour guide.

On the Saturday morning we had time for a quick walk along the banks of the Danube, just taking in the sights of Budapest. I was amazed at how many cruise boats there were in the river but sadly we didn't have time to jump on one.

Újpest kindly hosted a VIP lunch for us before their game with Debrecen on the Saturday afternoon and here I'm just about to make a little speech thanking Újpest for their excellent hospitality. I did mention that had we been on the losing side 50 years ago I'm not sure we would have been quite so gracious! I'm sure we would have but we were all really touched by their kind hosting of us.

Here I'm presenting Újpest captain, and my friend, Jonas Gorocs, with a current Newcastle United shirt. Jonas has just turned 80 but he still looked in good nick.

Also at the lunch I presented Újpest Managing Director Csaba Berta with a silver salver on behalf of Newcastle United to mark our 50 years of friendship. He told me the club were very honoured to host us and that the salver would take pride of place in their boardroom.

This picture was taken just as we arrived at the ground on Saturday lunchtime where we joined their former players on the pitch and it immediately brought the memories flooding back. Of course, it had changed a bit but it was definitely the ground where we lifted the cup!

Here are the four of us chatting with Antal Dunai who was one of their twin strikers I was up against when we played them. He and Ferenc Bene were a real handful and he wasn't shy of reminding me of that! Also pictured on the right is Matthew Watson-Broughton whose interpreting skills were invaluable.

The four of us in the Szusza Ferenc Stadion with a Újpest scarf presented to us by our hosts. I know it's only a minor thing, but it was nice that we were all dressed in suits with a club tie and badge. Very appropriate for the occasion.

Here I am with Újpest captain Jonas Gorocs, with the other lads looking on. It was so nice to exchange views on the two games we played. He said they didn't expect to lose 3-0 when they played the first leg in Newcastle and, also, when he scored the second goal just before half time in the second leg, they fully expected to go on and win the tie!

This was a picture taken just as we arrived at the ground, in front of their trophy cabinet in the reception area. They've won the League on 20 occasions and the Cup 10 times so you can imagine the trophy room was pretty well-stocked.

Here I am talking to goalkeeper Antal Szentimihalyi. I didn't mention the three goals I scored past him over the two legs, that would have been disrespectful to such a fine man. He told me about the years of success they enjoyed back in the 1960s and 1970s and how they were so bitterly disappointed to lose the final when they knew they had such a fine team back then.

It's just approaching kick off time at the Szusza Ferenc Stadion and the two teams, Újpest and Debrecen, line up for the traditional handshakes. Both teams needed to win to try and get third place in the league which would lead to a Europa League place in 2019/20 but predictably it ended 1-1.

We were asked to go down to the tunnel just before the half time whistle as when the Újpest and Debrecen players left the pitch, it was our cue to walk out on to the pitch to be greeted by the fans in the stadium. Following the PA announcement, the applause from all four sides of the ground was tremendous and it really made us feel greatly appreciated. A football suddenly appeared and an impromptu kick-about in the centre circle ensued. We were all a bit older but none of us had lost our touch.

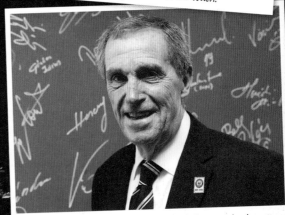

I'm pictured here with Alan Foggon just acknowledging the applause from the crowd as we walked onto the pitch.

Just me in this one, in the corridors leading down to the changing rooms. Újpest display various autograph boards of their players and here's just an example of one. Pretty good I thought.

We took this picture just before we were about to leave the stadium. I know it was 50 years ago but to be back in the stadium where we experienced what was undoubtedly one of the career highlights for all of us, if not the career highlight, was a fabulous experience for us all. For Alan, just looking towards the goal where he netted our third on the night was pretty emotional.

And finally it's the four of us pictured with the Újpest Press Officer Zambo Istvan (Steve to us in English) outside our hotel in the city centre, the Mercure. Steve organised everything for us and he could not have been a more friendly, enthusiastic and welcoming host.

This is the view from the top of Gellert Hill next to the daunting Freedom Statue that guards and over-looks the city. It afforded a magnificent panoramic view of Budapest.

CROSSWORD

ACROSS

2 Halloween night hat-trick hero. (5)

8 The conditions at the August 1999 game at St. James' Park. (7)

9 Sunderland player red-carded in the 5-1 hammering by United in 2010. (7)

10 Scored twice in United's 2-0 win in 2008 (4)

12 Scored his last United goal at Stadium of Light in 2006. (7)

14 Goalscoring Greek defender in 2002. (7)

15 Resigned after the 1999 defeat to Sunderland. (6)

16 Scored his only League goal against Sunderland in 2006. (5)

17 Saved a penalty in the 1990 play-offs. (8)

18 The last player to score in a Tyne-Wear derby. (8)

DOWN

1 United's manager in the 5-1 game in 2010. (7)

3 Scored 'that' free kick to win the game at Sunderland in 1992. (6)

4 The oddity at the game in Sunderland in September 1996. (2,4,4)

5 Scored after only three minutes at the Stadium of Light in 2012. (6)

6 He's nicknamed the 'Mackem Slayer'. (6)

7 United won 2-1 the last time the game was contested here in 1996. (5,4)

9 United hat-trick hero in the New Year's Day win in 1985. (9)

11 United 80s winger who played against the Magpies in 1997. (6)

13 United's all-time leading scorer against Sunderland. (7)

Answers can be found on page 62.

BBC Radio Newcastle have been commentating on the Magpies since the early 1990s. Many of you will remember Mick Lowes (right) bringing his very recognisable tones (and views) into the homes and cars of thousands of listeners throughout the region who weren't able to get to matches. They even brought out a cassette recording of the 1992/93 season, such was the interest in reliving the highlights of that memorable promotion campaign.

Mick filled the Radio Newcastle hot-seat for over 20 years (as well as having a stint with Metro Radio) but since December 2016, when he hung up his microphone, the role has passed seamlessly to the knowledgeable, perceptive and authoritatively-spoken **Matthew Raisbeck** who has successfully brought his own fresh perspective to the airwaves.

Here Matthew, who is joined at every game by summariser John Anderson, the former Republic of Ireland international with 337 United appearances behind him, takes us through a typical week covering the ups and downs of Newcastle United.

"The pre-match routine for a football commentator involves many hours of research. I spend my week preparing for the next match by looking at all sorts of information about Newcastle United. This includes studying the team's recent form and checking statistics about individual players such as how many appearances they have made and how many goals they have scored. And if there's any quirky or historical facts too, they're always very handy to have available as you never quite know when you're broadcasting live when you might use or need a particular line.

A couple of examples of Matthew's match notes.

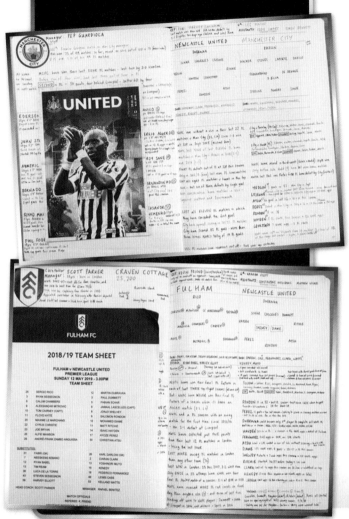

"The comments John and I make are always spontaneous, never rehearsed, as you never know what's going to happen next! We give our honest (and personal) opinions on what we see in front of us and I think our listeners appreciate that. We tell it as it is. If it's a poor game then the listeners need to know that or if there's a howler by one of the players, we're duty bound to be critical but never in a nasty way, more factual and supportive. After all we're as big supporters as the man or woman on the terrace or the fan listening at home.

"Obviously I'm well versed as far as Newcastle United is concerned but of course I have to familiarise myself with the opposition as well by writing down some facts about the team for example their recent results, and how to pronounce the names of their players – something that is very important! That's a tricky task as is being able to identify each opposing player as the game goes on, especially when you're watching from high up in the stand as we do at some away games. That's one essential task any commentator has to master and it's a skill you develop over time.

"If it's Manchester City at home then it's easy to say 'Sterling plays the ball out to Aguero' but if you're away at Macclesfield in the League Cup and one of their midfielders on the far side of the pitch puts over a deep cross, being able to quickly name him is an essential pre-requisite of good commentary.

"I put all this information into a big book that I take with me to each game and use different coloured pens to make sure the information stands out when I look down at my notes during the match.

"Every Friday before the weekend's game I get to interview the manager at the pre-match press conference. There aren't many better people to speak to about football than the boss of Newcastle United and if there is any news from the club, I will talk to him about that. Then, I will find out what he thinks about the game and ask if there are any injured players together with any other snippets of news I can gather.

"On the day of a match – whether it is at home or away - John Anderson and I are often the first members of the media to arrive at the stadium – yes, even before the manager and the players! We get there three hours before kick-off and immediately connect all our broadcasting equipment to the radio studio (to ensure it's all working properly), have something to eat, and then discuss what we are going to talk about during our hour-long programme before the action starts. The interview I did with the manager is always used in this segment, and if we have any player audio left over from a previous game that is relevant, then we might use that too.

"It's always nice to meet and chat with the radio presenters from other stations too, be it national stations like 5Live and talkSPORT, or our BBC colleagues working for the opposition.

"Once the referee gets the game under way, it is my job to describe what is happening - which team has possession of the ball, where the ball is on the pitch, if a goal is scored – and John, as our expert, is there to tell you whether it is good or bad! He also provides a tactical analysis when needed and of course, as a former player, can relate to specific incidents.

"Radio is about sounds – and there is no better sound than hearing St. James' Park roar when Newcastle have scored a goal! We have an extra microphone just for this to pick up the noise from the supporters. At appropriate points during the game, I will also mention some of the statistics and facts I have researched during the week, just so as to be as informative as possible for our listeners.

"And describing things like a player's hairstyle (Paul Dummett changed his midway through last season), the design of their boots, or even the weather, is also important because it allows us to bring you some of the colour of the game. Unlike television, there are no pictures on the radio, so we have to create those images.

"After the final whistle, we wait for the manager to come out of the dressing room to do his post-match interviews and we speak to some of the players as well in the mixed zone. If it's been a good result we might get up to three players but, conversely, a loss means we're normally happy with one and to be fair, the lads are always good enough to stop for us. I like to think there's a two-way respect there, we appreciate what they're doing on the pitch and they realise the job we have to do too.

"After the interviews are done (mainly using my phone) I send them back to the BBC Newcastle studio using an app – and they are played out on the radio so the fans can get instant reaction to the game, which I think is a really nice thing to be able to do.

"And finally, a little anecdote. Last season after we'd beaten Burnley 2-0 at St. James' Park, and Fabian Schär had scored a belter, we were keen to speak to him after the game but unfortunately he'd taken a knock and was still getting treatment in the changing room a good hour after the final whistle. We (myself and Lee Ryder from the Chronicle) thought we were thwarted but with the assistance of the Press Office, and with the approval of the club doctor, Fabian invited us into a deserted changing room where he was still in is kit, lying on the physio bench with an ice pack on his leg, to share his thoughts on the game, a gesture which we really appreciated."

SPOT THE DIFFERENCE

Can you spot the eight differences in this match between Newcastle and Manchester City?

The Newcastle United Foundation is the official charity of Newcastle United Football Club. It uses the local passion for football to inspire, encourage learning and promote healthy lifestyles, making a real difference to the lives of children, young people and families in the North East region.

Through its health, community education and coaching programmes, the Foundation has worked with almost 50,000 people across Newcastle, Gateshead, North Tyneside and Northumberland in the last year.

Here are a few pictures of some of the projects from last season, together with a number of other activities and events which the manager and players were involved with as part of their commitment to support the local community.

AYOZE PÉREZ VISITS BEECH HILL PRIMARY PUPILS

Former Magpies striker Ayoze Pérez surprised pupils at Beech Hill Primary School in the west end of the city when he joined them for their Premier League Primary Stars PE lesson. Foundation Ambassador Pérez donated a Premier League Primary Stars equipment pack, including footballs, numbered and lettered floor spots and giant dice, which teachers at the school could use in lessons across the curriculum to help inspire children to learn and be active. Pérez said: "Being active can be such fun and I was delighted to support this initiative."

CHRISTIAN ATSU GIVES THE BYKER COMMUNITY TRUST A DAY OUT AT NEWCASTLE UNITED

A group of young Byker residents got the opportunity of a lifetime as they travelled to Newcastle United's Training Ground for an incredible day out. The experience, initially donated by Newcastle United and Newcastle United Foundation to Christian Atsu's Black Star Dinner in aid of the charity 'Arms Around the Child', was offered to Foundation participants by the winning bidder, Bell Group. The day featured a front row seat to Newcastle United's first team training, before a very special training session with Atsu himself. Participants also got the chance to meet Magpies boss Rafa Benitez. Atsu said: "My charity work is very important to me both in Ghana and here in Newcastle and I was delighted to be able to help the Byker youngsters."

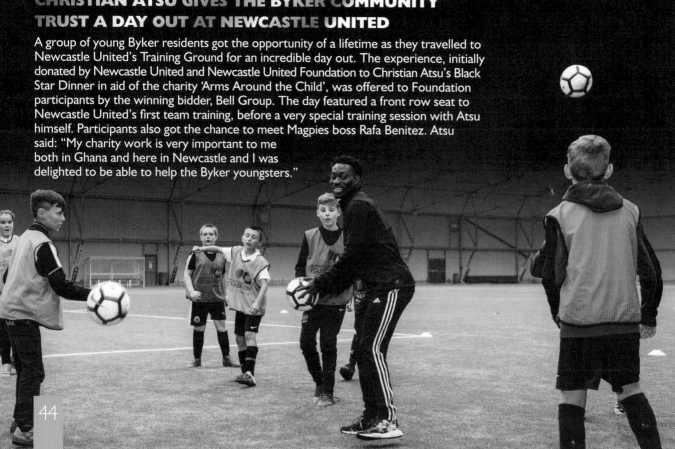

SEAN LONGSTAFF ANNOUNCED AS FOUNDATION AMBASSADOR

Newcastle United midfielder Sean Longstaff was unveiled as Newcastle United Foundation's newest Ambassador after making a guest appearance at the Great North Children's Hospital. Sean dropped in to meet children supported by an innovative programme delivered in partnership by Newcastle United Foundation with funding from the Sir Bobby Robson Foundation. The initiative delivers tailored sporting and education activities and programmes to young cancer patients, as well as providing support to their siblings and families. Sean said: "I am proud and privileged to be an ambassador for the Foundation, the work they do in the community is simply incredible."

DEANDRE YEDLIN SURPRISES BYKER SCHOOL PUPILS

DeAndre Yedlin met pupils at Byker Primary School to learn how the partnership between Newcastle United Foundation and Byker Community Trust is having a positive impact on the area. The United defender took the time to speak to the children and join in with the Foundation's activities on the day. Byker Community Trust funds a number of Newcastle United Foundation community programmes in the area. Yedlin said: "Coming to local primary schools is a very rewarding experience and if we as players can help in any way we're happy to do so. You could see on their faces the fun they were having and that really is the bottom line."

TOON FANS AT THE HEART OF NEW MENTAL HEALTH CAMPAIGN

Newcastle United Foundation launched a campaign encouraging Newcastle United fans to take a proactive approach to looking after their mental health. 'Be a Game Changer', funded by Newcastle City Council and the Premier League PFA Community Fund, aims to raise awareness, and change perception of mental health issues. The campaign encourages fans to take action to look after their mental health. The campaign has been supported by United players with Paul Dummett saying: "All the lads are very aware of mental health issues in football especially with there being a number of high profile cases recently reported. It's something we all take very seriously and as such we're right behind the campaign."

45

FREDDIE WOODMAN & JAMIE STERRY KICK OFF PREMIER LEAGUE ENTERPRISE

Newcastle United players Freddie Woodman and Jamie Sterry joined pupils from schools across the North East as the Premier League Enterprise Challenge heated up at St. James' Park. Foundation staff spent six weeks in schools working with pupils helping to develop their ideas and ensure their presentations covered the key areas of the programme. The United players took part in a Q&A session before joining a tour around the home changing room and pitch side. They then took centre stage as they presented the winning school, Joseph Swan Academy in Gateshead, with their prize. Joseph Swan Academy went on to reach the national final of the PL Enterprise challenge. Freddie said: "Huge congratulations to Joseph Swan Academy, they really immersed themselves in the challenge and were rewarded accordingly, well done to all who took part."

SALOMÓN RONDÓN GOES BACK TO SCHOOL WITH TESCO BANK

Venezuelan striker Salomón Rondón went back to school to launch the third year of Tesco Bank Junior Players at Collingwood Primary School in North Shields. The United number nine took the time to join in with the activities of the day, much to the delight of the budding young footballers. Tesco Bank Junior Players provided funding to give school children in the North East the opportunity to get fit and active by taking part in physical activity and receiving expert tuition from highly qualified coaches. Newcastle United Foundation delivered the programme to more than 5,000 primary school children in 2018/19. Rondón said: "The coaching the children receive through the Tesco programme will go a long way to shaping their development as they move through school, it's fantastic that we can help them in this way."

NEWCASTLE UNITED FOUNDATION 10-YEAR ANNIVERSARY DINNER

Newcastle United Foundation's 10 Year Anniversary fundraising dinner, raised a phenomenal £60,000 profit for the charity. The black-tie event, hosted by Gabby Logan, saw then-Newcastle United manager Rafa Benitez, alongside current and former players, join together to support the achievements of Foundation participants as well as celebrating a decade of the Foundation's community work. Former players Andy Cole and Frank Clark were inducted into the Newcastle United Hall of Fame at the star-studded event. Clark said: "It's a great honour to join the list of legendary Newcastle United names in the Hall of Fame. I am extremely grateful to the Foundation and am proud to be a supporter of the incredible work they do throughout the region."

BBC MATCH OF THE DAY VISITS UNITED'S 12th MAN PROGRAMME

Match of the Day visited Newcastle United's Training Ground to learn more about the Foundation's 12th Man programme. The initiative is a free 12-week healthy lifestyles programme for men aged between 30 and 65 who are looking to improve their physical and mental wellbeing. Players Joselu, Mo Diamé, Fabian Schär, and Jacob Murphy came along to get involved in the session, meet current and former 12th Man participants and hear how the programme has inspired them to make positive life changes. Schär said: "I like Match of the Day because they gave me 'Goal of the Month' but in all seriousness it was great for them to come and see our 12th Man Programme and it's nice that we're able to help improve the fitness of some of our older fans."

CHRISTMAS HOSPITAL VISITS

The visit to the local Newcastle hospitals is one of the highlights of the year for both the United players and staff as well as the children they meet whilst visiting the wards where they aim to bring some festive cheer to the children who are unfortunate enough to be hospitalised at this time of year. The Royal Victoria Infirmary, which houses the Great North Children's Hospital, is the main beneficiary of the visit and they also receive a cash donation from the players. Captain Jamaal Lascelles said: "The players really enjoy visiting the children but at the same time we realise how lucky we are to be fit and healthy. If we can bring just a little bit of joy to the children then it's worth more than you can ever imagine."

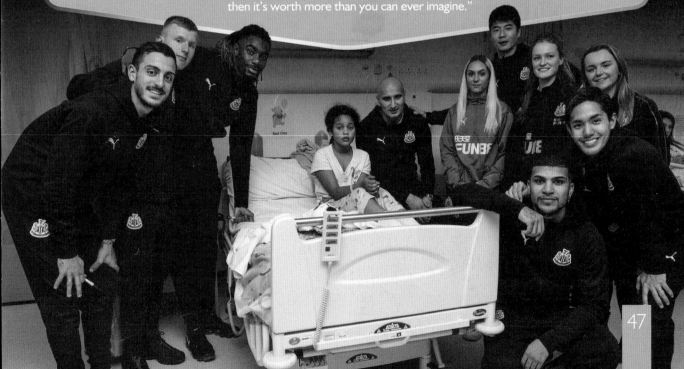

DeAndre Yedlin v Manchester City at the Etihad Stadium, 1 September 2018

Trailing to an early Raheem Sterling goal, in possibly their toughest away game of the season, half an hour had gone when Ki and Ayoze Pérez broke up a City attack just over halfway, Pérez angled a forward pass towards Kenedy who laid it off to the advancing Salomón Rondón before the Venezuelan threaded an excellent pass between John Stones and Aymeric Laporte which was hammered right-footed into the net from six yards out by DeAndre Yedlin who'd ran all the way from the halfway line. Great energy from the American and only his second United goal.

Kenedy v Manchester United at Old Trafford, 6 October 2018

With only two points on the board United incredibly raced into an early two-goal lead at Old Trafford, the first coming after only seven minutes. A throw in on the Newcastle right just inside their own half was played to Ayoze Pérez. With both Mutō and Kenedy making forward runs, he played a grass-cutter of a pass to the latter bisecting two defenders. The Brazilian took a touch to wrong-foot Ashley Young before stepping into the box and curling his shot inside the far post at the Stretford End of the ground. It was classy finish and put the pain of the Cardiff penalty miss behind him.

Fabian Schär v Cardiff City at St. James' Park, 19 January 2019

Needing a goal to break a stubborn Cardiff side down, midway through the first half Isaac Hayden found Fabian Schär wide on the right flank on the Milburn Stand side of the pitch just inside the Cardiff half. The Swiss defender pushed forward before heading for goal as the visiting defence more-or-less stood back and watched. Schär didn't panic and after seeing a shooting chance open up, he guided a low, looping left footer perfectly inside the far post and beyond the diving Neil Etheridge. Not a goal a defender would normally score but there again Fabian isn't your conventional centre-half.

Salomón Rondón v Manchester City at St. James' Park, 29 January 2019

Trailing to a goal scored after only 24 seconds, United were doing their utmost to find an equaliser against second placed Manchester City. With 66 minutes on the clock Matt Ritchie broke upfield on the left and his centre was headed out by Fernandinho but only to Isaac Hayden, who returned it goalwards for both Salomón Rondón and Christian Atsu to pursue it through a crowd of defenders. The Venezuelan forward got to it first and steered the ball into the ground from just outside the six yard box, seeing his effort bounce up and elude goalkeeper Ederson. Maybe a little scrappy but a goal of huge significance which set United up for their eventual winner.

Fabian Schär v Burnley at St. James' Park, 26 February 2019

Fabian Schär was rapidly showing himself as a defender who could comfortably operate in the final third of the field and when, on 24 minutes, he brought the ball forward down the United right and played it inside to Issac Hayden, there was no indication of what was to transpire 10 seconds later. Salomón Rondón picked up the pass but lost out to Jack Cork who could only clear as far as Javier Manquillo. Giving the ball back to Schär the Swiss defender strode forward before unleashing an unstoppable pile driver that flew in off the right Leazes upright as Clarets 'keeper Tom Heaton made a despairing dive. A sensational goal that deservedly won the BBC and Premier League Goal of the Month award.

49

Salomón Rondón v Everton at St. James' Park, 9 March 2019

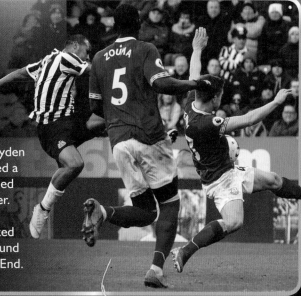

Trailing by two goals to Everton, United desperately needed some magic from somewhere. It arrived 25 minutes from time. A fine back-heel from Matt Ritchie inside the United half robbed Bernard and set Isaac Hayden away down the right. He picked out Pérez who directed a header back towards Rondón. The number nine returned the ball to Pérez, who had moved away from his marker. The Spaniard's next act was decisive; taking one touch with his right foot to make an angle before a superb flicked pass picked out Rondón, who had both feet off the ground when he memorably volleyed home at the Gallowgate End. Twenty-five minutes later United had won 3-2.

Salomón Rondón v Bournemouth at the Vitality Stadium, 16 March 2019

It was deep into first half injury time when Miguel Almirón strode forward with pace from inside his own half and only a cynical trip from behind by Jordon Ibe stopped his progress. With a few free-kick specialists on the pitch it was Salomón Rondón who grabbed the ball and he judged his 25-yard free-kick perfectly, curling it over the wall and into the top corner away from Artur Boruc. TV footage showed Matt Ritchie celebrating as the ball sailed over the wall - he knew where it was going from the moment it was hit!

Matt Ritchie v Bournemouth at the Vitality Stadium, 16 March 2019

And talking of Matt Ritchie here's a special one of his own. United were trailing 2-1 at the Vitality Stadium and were into the fifth minute of a minimum of three added on. Paul Dummett's hopeful punt forward was headed out weakly and reached Florian Lejeune, who directed it to DeAndre Yedlin on the right. The defender hit a looping cross that looked initially destined for Rondón but fell in front of Matt Ritchie on the left edge of the box. He caught it beautifully and half-volleyed the ball left-footed into the roof of the net. Absolutely unstoppable and a reminder of the goal he scored at the same end for the Cherries against Sunderland back in September 2015 – a better goal than this one Matt said but only just.

Ayoze Pérez v Brighton at the Amex Stadium, 26 April 2019

United had already secured their Premier League status by the time they travelled to face Chris Hughton's Seagulls at the Amex in the last week of April, by contrast Albion were still in need of a point or two. Just after the half hour mark Paul Dummett's cross to the far post was chested down by Salomón Rondón into the path of Ayoze Pérez who lashed the ball into the top corner from 15 yards at the North End of the ground – the same end where he had scored back in February 2017 when his goal proved absolutely crucial in eventually securing the Championship for the Magpies.

Jonjo Shelvey v Fulham at Craven Cottage, 12 May 2019

The final game of the season and a lovely sunny day on the banks of the Thames. After only nine minutes a clever Matt Ritchie corner from the right found Jonjo Shelvey on the right side of the area. He controlled the ball before dispatching a fabulous dipping volley into the far corner of the net at the Hammersmith End of the ground. Pursued by Messrs Hayden, Schär and Lascelles, the scorer ran to the opposite end of the ground where his celebrations in front of the away fans were intense to say the least, clenched fist salutes and kiss blowing rounded off by the 'binocular' gesture seen previously from him.

Newcastle United, as members of the Premier League, are big business not only in the UK but right around the world. In this article we've pulled together some interesting facts and figures, related both to Newcastle United and the Premier League in general, which illustrates just how much football influences our lives on and off the pitch.

* 971,297 fans attended the 19 Premier League games at St. James' Park in 2018/19 at an average of 51,121 – and that's 98% capacity. Across the board, for the seventh season in a row, Premier League stadiums were more than 95% full.

* Combine that with the Global reach of the Premier League, and the Magpies will find their way into more than 1 billion households this season (2019/20).

* Newcastle United have a social media following of more than 3.7m.

* The Premier League is the most popular league in the majority of key international markets, delivering the highest levels of interest out of major European leagues. These markets include the USA, Australia, India and South Africa.

* In 2018/19, there were 1,072 goals scored, the highest on record in a 20-team Premier League Season. Salomón Rondón (above) scores the 1,071st goal of last season at Fulham.

* Last season former United midfielder James Milner became the 13th player to reach 500 Premier League appearances.

* Last season (2018/19), there was a 10.2% increase on average live TV audiences in the UK compared to 2017/18.

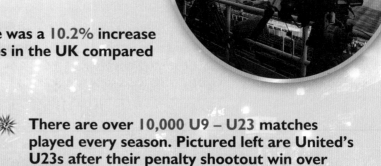

* There are over 10,000 U9 – U23 matches played every season. Pictured left are United's U23s after their penalty shootout win over Macclesfield.

* There were over 6.3m managers in the Fantasy Premier League… that's more than the population of New Zealand!

✳ **Over 79% of Primary schools in England (16,400) engaged in the Premier League's Primary Stars education project.**

✳ **Over 12,000 participants took part in the PL/BT Disability programme sessions in 2018/19 and there are over 500,000 participants in community projects each season.**

✳ **Over 25,000 coaches and referees were trained by the Premier League skills programme.**

✳ **Over 68% of people polled thought the Premier League makes them think better of the UK.**

✳ **The Premier League is watched in over 190 countries worldwide.**

✳ **The Premier League and its clubs fund community facilities across England and Wales via the Football Foundation and, since its inception nearly 20 years ago, 3,853 community pitches have been provided.**

✳ **69 clubs across the UK have delivered the Premier League Kicks programme which uses the power of football to bring communities together and engage with young people.**

✳ **There are players from 63 different countries in the Premier League. Pictured below is Paraguay's Miguel Almirón.**

✳ **Newcastle United makes a substantial economic contribution to the North East region. The total GVA (gross value) is £236m, there's an £89m tax contribution and over 2000 jobs are supported.**

✳ **Matchdays, conferences and special events offer a significant boost to the North of Tyne visitor economy. Almost one fifth of the fans who attend matches at St. James' Park over the course of a season live abroad or outside the north east region. There are 13,400 international fan visits, 174,600 rest of the UK domestic fan visits, and there is £21m of visitor spending.**

Well the answer is yes! There are plenty of interesting and informative miscellaneous facts and figures about Newcastle United so we thought we'd share a few of them with you in this fun to read article.

QUICKEST GOALS

Newcastle United have scored three goals inside the first minute in their 920 Premier League matches to the end of season 2018/19). The list below shows all goals (in seconds) scored in the first two minutes of games.

Kenedy (2018)

January 2003 Manchester City (H) Alan Shearer	10
January 1996 Arsenal (H) David Ginola	56
March 2004 Charlton Athletic (H) Alan Shearer	57
Machr 2018 Southampton (H) Kenedy	64
April 2006 Tottenham (H) Lee Bowyer	66
February 2009 West Brom (A) Damien Duff	67
February 2006 Aston Villa (A) Shola Ameobi	74
September 2002 Sunderland (H) Craig Bellamy	84
February 2011 Birmingham City (A) Peter Løvenkrands	95
August 1997 Sheff Wednesday (H) Tino Asprilla	98
January 2013 Everton (H) Papiss Cissé	111
November 2013 Norwich (H) Loïc Rémy	113
September 2007 West Ham (H) Mark Viduka	117

Cissé (2013)

GOALSCORING DEBUTS IN THE PREMIER LEAGUE

Georginio Wijnaldum was the last of seven players to make a goalscoring debut for the club in the Premier League. The number in brackets is the time on the pitch in minutes before scoring (Cissé and Mathie did so from the bench). Interestingly all were at St. James' Park.

1 Alex Mathie v Sheff Wed (H) 1993 (19 mins)
2 Les Ferdinand v Coventry City (H) 1995 (83 mins)
3 Stephane Guivarc'h v Liverpool (H) 1998 (28 mins)
4 Duncan Ferguson v Wimbledon (H) 1998 (59 mins)
5 Xisco v Hull City (H) 2008 (82 mins)
6 Papiss Cissé v Aston Villa (H) 2012 (57 mins)
7 Georginio Wijnaldum v Southampton (H) 2015 (48 mins)

HAT-TRICK HEROES

Ayoze Pérez was the 11th player to have scored a Premier League treble for Newcastle (v Southampton in April 2019) and his was the 14th hat-trick completed by those 11 players (again to the end of the 2018/19 season). And of the 14, all but two were scored at St. James' Park.

1993/94 Peter Beardsley v Wimbledon (H)
1993/94 Andy Cole v Liverpool (H)
1993/94 Andy Cole v Coventry City (H)
1995/96 Les Ferdinand v Wimbledon (H)
1996/97 Alan Shearer v Leicester City (H)
1999/00 Alan Shearer v Sheffield Wednesday (H) (5)
2005/06 Michael Owen v West Ham (A)
2010/11 Andy Carroll v Aston Villa (H)
2010/11 Kevin Nolan v Sunderland (H)
2010/11 Leon Best v West Ham (H)
2011/12 Demba Ba v Blackburn Rovers (H)
2011/12 Demba Ba v Stoke City (H)
2015/16 Georginio Wijnaldum v Norwich City (H) (4)
2018/19 Ayoze Pérez v Southampton (H)

Conversely, 14 players (two of them twice) have scored hat tricks against United in the Premier League era:

Teddy Sheringham (Tottenham 1994)
Dwight Yorke (Aston Villa 1996)
Michael Owen (Liverpool 1998)
Andy Cole (Manchester Utd 1999)
Ray Parlour (Arsenal 2000)
Michael Owen (Liverpool 2001)
Ruud van Nistelrooy (Manchester Utd 2002)
Paul Scholes (Manchester Utd 2003)
Cristiano Ronaldo (Manchester Utd 2008)
John Carew (Aston Villa 2008)
Somen Tchoyi (West Brom 2011)
Clint Dempsey (Tottenham 2012)
Theo Walcott (Arsenal 2012)
Eden Hazard (Chelsea 2014)
Sergio Aguero (Manchester City 2015
Sergio Aguero (Manchester City 2018)

PLAYED FOR and SCORED AGAINST UNITED

Ryan Taylor

There are 33 players who have played for Newcastle in the Premier League but have also scored against Newcastle in the Premier League.

Craig Bellamy, Lee Bowyer, Michael Bridges, Lee Clark, Jack Colback, Andy Cole, Carl Cort, Duncan Ferguson, Damien Duff, Les Ferdinand, Abdoulaye Faye, Kevin Gallacher, Dwight Gayle, Geremi, Darren Huckerby, Didi Hamann, Stephen Ireland, Ronny Johnsen, Paul Kitson, Lomana LuaLua, Kevin Nolan, Charles N'Zogbia, Michael Owen, Gavin Peacock, Loic Remy, Wayne Routledge, Ian Rush, Louis Saha, Alan Shearer, Gary Speed, Alan Smith, Ryan Taylor, Mark Viduka.

THEY SHARE THE SAME NAME

There are 11 sets of players with same surname who have played for United in the Premier League era:

Ameobi (Shola and Sammy)

Barton (Warren and Joey)

Campbell (Adam and Sol)

Clark (Lee and Ciaran)

De Jong (Siem and Luuk)

Faye (Abdoulaye and Amady)

Ferguson (Duncan and Shane)

LuaLua (Lomana and Kazenga)

O'Brien (Liam, Andy and Alan)

Robinson (Mark and Paul)

Taylor (Steven and Ryan)

But only three were brothers, the Ameobis, LuaLuas and De Jongs. There were other brothers at the club in the last 30 years, e.g. the Caldwell's and the Appleby's but only one played Premier League football, Steve and Matty respectively.

Joey Barton

Warren Barton

MORE THAN 10?

There have been seven games in United's history when the total amount of goals scored in the game has exceeded 10!

October 1946 Newport County (H)	won 13-0
March 1928 Aston Villa (H)	won 7-5
January 1934 Liverpool (H)	won 9-2
Sepember 1930 Manchester United (A)	won 7-4
December 1909 Liverpool (A)	lost 5-6
September 1958 Chelsea (A)	lost 5-6
November 1930 Portsmouth (H)	lost 4-7

Albert Shepherd scored four at Anfield in 1909 but United still lost 6-5.

THEY ONLY PLAYED ONCE

In the Premier League era, 231 players have represented Newcastle United up until the end of the 2018/19 season – and of those 231 there are eight who only played one game!

Ivan Toney	Matty Appleby
Martin Brittain	James Coppinger
Darren Huckerby	Brian Kilcline (right)
Jamie Sterry	Antonio Barreca

AND TO FINISH...

...Here are a few odds and ends:

The team United have played more times than any other?
Arsenal, 183 matches

The team United have scored most goals against?
Aston Villa, 245 goals

The team United have beaten most times?
Manchester City, 72 wins

Two players with over 300 Premier League appearances for United?
Shay Given (354) and Alan Shearer (303)

The manager to have overseen the most Premier League games?
Bobby Robson (188)

And finally, there are eight current League teams Newcastle have never played:

Crawley, Fleetwood, Forest Green, Macclesfield, MK Dons, Rochdale, Salford and Wycombe

TWENTY FIVE YEARS OF PREMIER LEAGUE FOOTBALL

Newcastle United have just begun their 25th season in the Premier League and, at the start of the 2019/20 campaign, were the eighth most successful team in the competition's history. Here, we pick out a pictorial highlight from each season, a magic moment that will always provide a fond and enduring memory for United fans all around the world.

1993/94

Andy Cole sets a new goal-scoring record for United when he breaks the 40-goal barrier against Aston Villa at St. James' Park in April 1994. United won 5-1 and in their maiden Premier League campaign the Magpies finished the season in an excellent third place.

1994/95

United's 3-2 win at Arsenal was their sixth in a row at the start of the season in an unbeaten start to the campaign that lasted 11 matches. The goals came from Peter Beardsley (2) and Ruel Fox. United led the table until mid-November but tailed off to finish sixth. Off the pitch Andy Cole was sold to Manchester United.

1995/96

There are debuts for David Ginola, Les Ferdinand, Warren Barton and Shaka Hislop as United beat Coventry City 3-0 on the opening day of the season at a remodelled 36,500 capacity St. James' Park. Sadly, the Premier League title just eluded the Magpies that season.

1996/97

United sign Alan Shearer for a world record £15m from Blackburn Rovers. The Magpies beat Manchester United 5-0 at St. James' Park in October 1996 to record what was probably their most memorable Premier League victory of all time. Here Philippe Albert has just scored United's fifth, a glorious lob over keeper Peter Schmeichel.

1997/98

United reached the FA Cup Final and played in the Champions League but, in the League, there were few highlights as the Magpies finished a lowly 13th. Pictured here is Tino Asprilla scoring the first of his two goals to beat Sheffield Wednesday in August 1997.

1998/99

Ruud Gullit takes over at the helm but there's another FA Cup Final defeat and another below par season of Premier League football repeating the finishing position of the previous season. The highlight? Probably scoring an aggregate of nine goals against Coventry City, winning 4-1 at home and 5-1 away.

1999/00

There can only be one memory to show this season and it's not Ruud Gullit's United losing to Sunderland in the rain. At least that hastened the arrival of Bobby Robson and, in his first home game, Alan Shearer bagged five goals as the Magpies tore Sheffield Wednesday to shreds, winning 8-0.

2000/01

Over 51,000 in the newly enlarged St. James' Park, the Milburn and Gallowgate stands increasing in capacity, roared United to a first home game victory over Derby County. It finished 3-2 to the Geordies with debut goals from Carl Cort and Daniel Cordone, and a third from Stephen Glass.

2001/02

There was a classic encounter with Manchester United early in the season which saw the Magpies win 4-3 but we're going with another 4-3, this time the away win over Leeds United at Elland Road just before Christmas. Nobby Solano scored a last minute winner, a result that kept Newcastle at the summit of the Premier League after their midweek win at Highbury.

2002/03

There was more dramatic Champions League action for United as they qualified for the second group phase but domestically, Alan Shearer's goal against Manchester City, after only 10 seconds, was beaten only by the goal even he considers to be his best – his stunning dipping volley against Everton.

2003/04

A solid fifth place finish in the League was little consolation for missing out on matches against Real Madrid and AC Milan in the Champions League but there were a number of terrific performances and goals with maybe the pick being the 4-0 home win over Tottenham and two magical Laurent Robert strikes.

2004/05

United had decent runs in both the FA Cup and UEFA Cup but finished a disappointing 14th in the League under Graeme Souness. The most exciting game of the campaign came early in the season when Manchester City were the visitors to Tyneside. Incredibly, after a goalless first half, a seven-goal thriller was just edged by United. Don't mention the Bowyer/Dyer incident against Aston Villa though.

2005/06

Quite a few landmarks this season and the record signing of Michael Owen. Alan Shearer equalled and then passed the legendary Jackie Milburn's scoring record, finishing with a club record 206 goals but maybe his lasting memory was the celebration after banging in his final goal against Sunderland at the Stadium of Light.

2006/07

What do you remember most about the 2006/07 season? Probably not a great deal. A promising UEFA Cup run was ended in the Last 16 by AZ Alkmaar whilst a 2-1 home victory over Liverpool was commendable. Step forward recent Champions League winner James Milner as his New Year's Day blockbuster against Manchester United was undoubtedly the goal of the season.

2007/08

An unusual season, half managed by Sam Allardyce and half by the returning Kevin Keegan. Manchester United beat us by a combined score of 11-1, how embarrassing was that, but maybe the only real highlight was the Gallowgate beating of old foes Sunderland with Michael Owen getting a brace, the first, a header after only four minutes.

2008/09

United fell through the dreaded relegation trapdoor in May 2009 so there wasn't much to shout about. Maybe the last-minute win over Tottenham just before Christmas, or the late season win over Middlesbrough that gave the Geordies hope, under the management of Alan Shearer who came in for the last eight games of the season. Sadly though, it was to no avail.

2010/11

Back in the Premier League at the first time of asking, United opened their home campaign by hitting six past Aston Villa with Andy Carroll getting a hat-trick. But it didn't get any better than the Halloween massacre of Sunderland, the Magpies winning 5-1 at a joyous St. James' Park with Kevin Nolan getting a treble and Shola Ameobi two.

2011/12

Under the management of Alan Pardew United were unbeaten in their first 11 games, reaching a high of third place, and went on to finish fifth in the League, qualifying for the following season's UEFA Cup. Home wins over Manchester United and Liverpool were the stand-out occasions of a very enjoyable season.

2012/13

United reached the quarter-finals of the UEFA Cup, losing narrowly to Benfica, which may have contributed to their lowly 16th place finish. The 3-2 home win over Chelsea was a high point, with newly signed French recruits giving the team a valuable boost, whilst United's longest serving player, Steve Harper, bowed out against Arsenal after 20 years at St. James' Park.

2013/14

A pretty consistent campaign with United staying in the top half of the table from October onwards, despite only winning one of their last eight games. Four straight wins in November, which earned Alan Pardew the Manager of the Month award, was the standout point of the season with the 2-0 home win over Champions League semi-finalists Chelsea, most notable.

2014/15

United beat Everton in their last game of 2014 to move up to ninth in the table but then a paltry two wins in their next 18 games saw them need a last day of the season win over West Ham at St. James' Park to ensure Premier League survival. With John Carver holding the fort after Alan Pardew had departed early in the New Year, goals from Moussa Sissoko and Jonás Gutiérrez did the trick.

2015/16

It was nine games into the season before United recorded their first win of the campaign, and that an amazing 6-2 win over Norwich featuring a Gini Wijnaldum four-goal salvo. Of course that was relegation form and the Magpies were doomed before their final game of the season against Tottenham. Incredibly, in front of a delirious capacity crowd, United hammered the Londoners 5-1 with a delighted Rafa Benítez in the manager's hotseat.

2017/18

As they had done in 2010, United bounced back into the Premier League at the first time of asking and after the first five games were in an unlikely fourth place. That couldn't last of course, but an end of season tenth place finish was hugely respectable. Beating Manchester United at home, which sparked a run of four straight Gallowgate wins, was undoubtedly a key point in the season.

2018/19

United are often described as a 'roller-coaster' club and this season was no different to many before it. Bottom of the table in October, FA Cup dreams dashed when there was hope of a decent run in the competition, beating the eventual League Champions (the last club to do so) and crowds averaging over 51,000 yet again at St. James' Park.

The 25th season of Premier League football at St. James' Park is now upon us, and who knows what that will bring...

2019/20

Quiz One – page 21

1. Fabian Schär
2. Wolverhampton Wanderers
3. Martin Dúbravka
4. Isaac Hayden & DeAndre Yedlin
5. Cardiff, Fulham & Huddersfield
6. Liverpool (7)
7. Burnley
8. Antonio Barreca
9. FC Augsburg
10. Manchester United

Quiz Two – page 21

1. Swindon Town
2. Peter Beardsley
3. Coventry City
4. Shay Given
5. Pavel Srnicek
6. 1995/96
7. 13th
8. Liverpool
9. Georginio Wijnaldum
10. Nottingham Forest

Spot the Ball – page 23

Southampton match

Tottenham match

Crossword – page 39

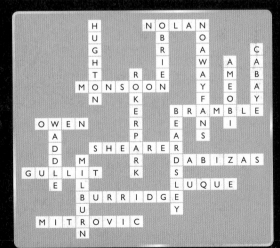

Spot the Difference – page 43